Contents

Hubble Bubble

A POTENT BREW OF MAGICAL POEMS

compiled by

ANDREW FUSEK PETERS

illustrated by

MELANIE WILLIAMSON

First published in Great Britain in 2003 by Hodder Wayland,
an imprint of Hodder Children's Books.

10 9 8 7 6 5 4 3 2 1

Editor: Kay Barnham
Designer: Jane Hawkins

British Library Cataloguing in Publication Data
Hubble Bubble
    1. Witches – Juvenile poetry 2. Wizards – Juvenile poetry
    3. Magic – Juvenile poetry 4. Children's poetry, English
    I. Peters, Andrew, 1965–
    821'.008'037

ISBN 0 7502 4118 7

Printed and bound in Great Britain by Clays Ltd, St Ives plc.

Hodder Children's Books
A division of Hodder Headline Limited
338 Euston Road, London NW1 3BH

Hubble Bubble

A POTENT BREW OF MAGICAL POEMS

Foreword

Welcome to *Hubble Bubble* – a collection of magical poems to make you laugh out loud, scare you witless or totally bewitch you. Look out for old favourites by Shakespeare, Ben Jonson and Keats as well as contemporary poems from top children's writers including Pauline Fisk, Helen Dunmore and Paul Cookson.

Hubble Bubble is divided into sections so you can find just what you're looking for:

Witches and Wizards begins with a poem about Merlin's football skills by Paul Cookson (page 9) and includes a ghoulish extract from Shakespeare's *Macbeth* (page 25).

Magic and Magicians features David Bateman's hilarious *Matchbox* (page 34) and the truly magical *Asking The Hare* by Helen Dunmore (page 42).

Ghosts, Ghouls and Goblins wouldn't be complete without Christina Rossetti's *Goblin Market* (page 54). But beware Patricia Leighton's baked bean imp... (page 80).

In **Myths and Legends**, fly away on the wings of Debjani Chatterjee's *Vishnu's Eagle* (page 86).

Twilight includes Brian Moses' wonderful *Feather from an Angel* (page 128) – prepare to be enchanted...

The final section is packed with **Curses, Charms and Spells** and includes *Spell* (page 150) by Bruce Barr – a great writer who inspired me and taught me my craft. This book is dedicated to him.

Andrew Fusek Peters

1
WITCHES
and WIZARDS

Wizard with the Ball

Young Arthur Merlin's spellbinding
His skills are crystal clear
A wizard with the ball
He makes it disappear!

Which is very useful in the opposition's penalty area.

Paul Cookson

Hell's Angel?

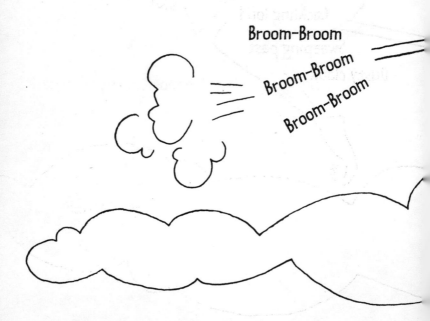

Broom-Broom

Broom-Broom

Broom-Broom

Greasy hair
Bristly chin
Sharp helmet
Evil grin

Revving fast
Cackling loud
Sweeping past
Dusty cloud

Philip Waddell

The **Wizard** and the **Lizard**

Once a wizard in a blizzard
Caught a lizard down a well
First he took it, then he shook it,
Did he cook it? Time will tell.

How he stuttered as he muttered,
Till he spluttered out a spell.
Then, hey presto! Full of zest-o.
Have you guessed? O do not yell!

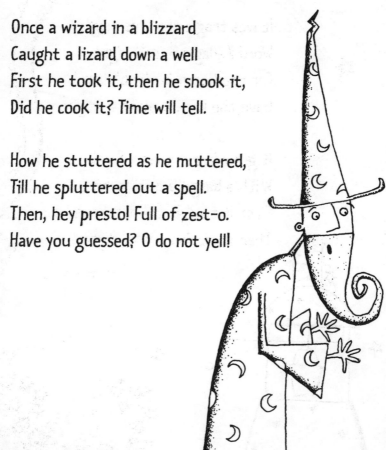

It was tragic that his magic
Word Kadagic wasn't right;
For the lizard in the blizzard
Gave the wizard quite a fright.

It grew larger than a Rajah,
With a barge, a butt, a bite;
First it fizzled, till it grizzled,
Then it sizzled out of sight.

Colin West

13

An Autumn Ghost

I am the ghost of the broomstick
Old Jinny Green Teeth rode.

On autumn days you hear me
Sweeping leaves down the road.

It's what always happens to broomsticks
When their witches are dead,

They become the winds of autumn
Whistling round your head.

Matt Simpson

Haiku

At the witching hour...
the screeching wheels of hamsters...
running for their lives!

Philip Waddell

Buckle Shoe Dance

Witch, twitch, grimbleclitch,
Stir up the cauldron with a switch
Cleaved from an elm at dead of night,
Seared by the moon to bright, bone white.

Call up your sisters, bid them prance,
Skirts a-swirl to the buckle shoe dance,
Skinny knuckle fingers patterning the air,
Clatter crack spike nails twist and tear.

Heel toe scrunch on rustle dry leaves,
Banshee cackle as the snake dance weaves.
Cobwebs drift where shadows lie,
To clutch at a witch as she swishes by.

Witch, twitch, grimbleclitch,
Stir up the cauldron with a switch,
Cleaved from an elm at dead of night,
Seared by the moon to bright, bone, white.

Shirley Tomlinson

Witches Gather

Dame, dame! The watch is set:
Quickly come, we all are met.
From the lakes and from the fens,
From the rocks and from the dens,
From the woods and from the caves,
From the churchyards, from the graves,
From the dungeon, from the tree
That they die on, here are we!

The weather is fair, the wind is good:
Up, dame, on your horse of wood!
Or else tuck up your grey frock,
And saddle your goat or your green cock,
And make his bridle a ball of thread
To toll up how many miles you have rid.
Quickly come away,
For we all stay.

The owl is abroad, the bat and the toad,
  And so is the cat-a-mountain;
The ant and the mole sit both in a whole,
  And the frog peeps out of the fountain.
The dogs they do bay, and the timbrels play,
  The spindle is now a-turning;
The moon it is red, and the stars are fled,
  But the sky is a-burning

Ben Jonson

The Sorceror's Dentist

The Sorceror went to the dentist,
She welcomed him in with a grin;
But she wasn't his usual dentist,
She was only filling in.

'filling in'... get it? She was only fill...
Oh, suit yourself!

She took the Sorceror's tooth out,
Which quite annoyed the chap,
Especially when the dentist said,
'Remember to "Mind The Gap" '.

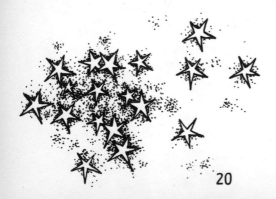

'Mind The Gap!' It's a pun, see?
'Cos on the London Underground...
Oh, forget it!

The Sorceror put a spell on her;
Now up and down the hill
The dentist marches day and night,
Like a soldier doing the drill.

'drill'... come on, you must get that one.
Oh, go and write your own poems.

Mike Jubb

From

Tam O'Shanter – A Tale

She ventured forward on the light;
And, vow! Tam saw an unco sight!
Warlocks and witches in a dance;
Nae cotillion brent new frae France,
But hornpipes, jigs, strathspeys, and reels,
Put life and mettle in their heels.
A winnock-bunker in the east,
There sat auld Nick, in shape o'beast;
A towzie tyke, black, grim, and large,
To gie them music was his charge:
He screw'd the pipes, and gart them skirl,
Till roof and rafters a' did dirl. –
Coffins stood round, like open presses,
That shaw'd the dead in their last dresses;
And by some devilish cantraip slight
Each in its cauld hand held a light.

Robert Burns

The Ride-by-nights

Up on their brooms the Witches stream,
Crooked and black in the crescent gleam;
One foot high, and one foot low,
Bearded, cloaked, and cowled, they go.
'Neath Charlie's Wain they twitter and tweet,
And away they swarm 'neath the Dragon's feet,
With a whoop and a flutter they swing and sway,
And surge pell-mell down the Milky Way.
Between the legs of the glittering Chair
They hover and squeak in the empty air.
Then round they swoop past the glimmering Lion
To where Sirius barks behind huge Orion;
Up, then, and over to wheel amain,
Under the silver, and home again.

Walter de la Mare

A Country Spell Against Witches

Blackthorn bark and poppy seed,
Thistle down and water-weed,
Send the witches off with speed.

Jennifer Curry

From **Macbeth**

(From Act I, Scene IV)

MACBETH:
  I conjure you, by that which you profess,
  Howe'er you come to know it, answer me –
  Though you untie the winds and let them fight
  Against the churches; though the yesty waves
  Confound and swallow navigation up;
  Though bladed corn be lodged and trees blown down;
  Though castles topple on their warders' heads;
  Though palaces and pyramids do slope
  Their heads to their foundations; though the treasure
  Of nature's germens tumble all together
  Even till destruction sicken – answer me
  To what I ask you.

FIRST WITCH:

Round about the cauldron go;
In the poisoned entrails throw:
Toad that under cold stone
Days and nights has thirty-one.
Sweltered venom, sleeping got,
Boil thou first i'the charmèd pot.

ALL:

Double, double, toil and trouble;
Fire burn, and cauldron bubble.

SECOND WITCH:

Fillet of a fenny snake
In the cauldron boil and bake;
Eye of newt, and toe of frog,
Wool of bat, and tongue of dog,
Adder's fork, and blind-worm's sting,
Lizard's leg and howlet's wing,
For a charm of powerful trouble,
Like a hell-broth, boil and bubble.

ALL:

Double, double, toil and trouble;
Fire burn, and cauldron bubble.

William Shakespeare

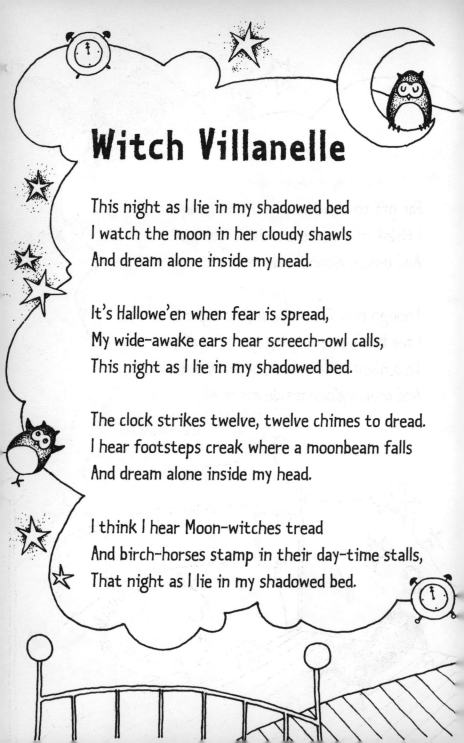

Witch Villanelle

This night as I lie in my shadowed bed
I watch the moon in her cloudy shawls
And dream alone inside my head.

It's Hallowe'en when fear is spread,
My wide-awake ears hear screech-owl calls,
This night as I lie in my shadowed bed.

The clock strikes twelve, twelve chimes to dread.
I hear footsteps creak where a moonbeam falls
And dream alone inside my head.

I think I hear Moon-witches tread
And birch-horses stamp in their day-time stalls,
That night as I lie in my shadowed bed.

Far off to the dark wood the moon has fled.
I think of a tattered witch and trolls
And dream alone inside my head.

Though now from the sky no light is shed,
I see black cats leaping garden walls,
This night as I lie in my shadowed bed
And dream alone inside my head.

Catherine Benson

Wizard and Witch

I am the egg, and I will imprison you.
I am the bird, and I will thrust for life.
But I am a cage; I shall see you pine away.
I am a feather, drawn out on the wind.
Now I'm black tar, and I will weigh you down.
I will be sunshine, to melt you and run free.
I will be fog, to choke you and confuse.
My rains will come, dissolving you to dew.
Ah, but my river will swallow your every drop.
I am a fish, and I will leap your dams.

But not my fine net, to hold you alive or dead.

See, as pearls I drop down through your mesh.

Pierced and necklaced I hold you on my thread.

But I glance away from you in moonlight sparks.

My chimney holds your sparks and turn them to soot.

My cold heart freezes and turns me to snowflakes.

My hands will pack you into a snowball.

But when you fling me I will scatter as birds do.

I am the egg, and I will imprison you.

David Duncombe
and Berlie Doherty

2
MAGIC and
MAGICIANS

You'll like this, not a lot!

I once saw a magician
Who had the weird habit.
Of pulling a top hat
Out of his rabbit!

Steve Fisher

Matchbox

Here is a matchbox.
What is in a matchbox? you ask.
Matches, perhaps?
No, not matches.
Something much better.
Something magic
Something wonderful.
Come up close and I will show you.

Are you ready?
Right
There!

Oh.
It is full of matches.
I am sorry,
I seem to have brought the wrong matchbox.

Perhaps tomorrow.

David Bateman

The Magician's Hands

Fly at light-speed.
He can make you believe
In make-believe —
That the Queen of Hearts
Is a turtle dove,
That an egg can open
To a bouquet of flowers.

As the coloured scarves
Rainbow endlessly
From his mouth,
You hang on the cliff
Edge of wonder.

Watch. Watch him
Very carefully.
Your imagination
Is the only thing he has
Up his sleeve.

J Patrick Lewis

The Magician

The magician at Daphne's party
Was called The Great Zobezank
But we knew it was only Daphne's dad
Who worked at the Westminster Bank.

He waved his wand and told us all,
'I need a volunteer
Who'll step inside my magic box
And mysteriously disappear.'

We shouted, 'Mister, hey mister, please choose me'
And waved our arms like mad
But he choose Daphne Smartyboots
Because he was her dad.

He raised his little magic wand
And waved it in the air
And when he opened his magic box
Daphne wasn't there.

He bowed and smiled, while Daphne's mum
Shouted 'Bravo' and cheered
Then Zobezank shouted the magic words
To make Daphne re-appear.

But when he opened the magic door
No Daphne stood inside
And her father muttered, 'Oh deary me'
While her mother wailed and cried.

They called, 'Oh Daphne, dear, where are you?'
And beat upon the door
But as for us we clapped and cheered
Louder than before.

Gareth Owen

Abracadabra Alphabet

The Alchemist artfully searches for gold,
The Banshee balefully wails in the cold,
The Changeling chillingly grins in his basket,
The Dragon dreamily coils round his casket,
The Elves enchantingly dance through the sky,
The Fairy-Folk fiercely flicker and fly,
The Gorgon girlishly tosses her hair,
The Hag-Wife horribly lurks in her lair,
The Imp ingeniously leaps over walls,
The Jackdaw jeeringly curses and calls,
The Knights unknowingly sip from the Grail,
The Lamia lovingly rattles each scale,
The Mermaid mournfully sobs in the sea,
The Wood-Nymphs naughtily hide in a tree,

The Ogre odiously batters the door,
The Pentangle palely patterns the floor,
The Quill-Pen quizzically scribbles a spell,
The Runes repeatedly twist what they tell,
The Sirens saucily sing their sweet song,
The Troll titanically thunders along,
The Unicorn urgently gallops away,
The Vampire viciously punctures his prey,
The Werewolf wickedly sets out to scare,
Excalibur expertly slices the air,
The Yeti yawningly blunders around,

AND...

The Zombies lazily snooze underground.

Clare Bevan

Magic Mat

I took my magic carpet
Into the laundromat
I should have read the label
Now it's a magic mat

Roger Stevens

Alchemy

Throw in metal,
stuff that's old.
The object is
to make some gold.

Cans with ring pulls,
broken tools.
We must all be
proper fools.

What we've got's
a landfill site,
brewing trouble
out of sight.

Throw in metal.
What's it worth
when you've mixed up
the whole Earth?

Jill Townsend

Asking the Hare

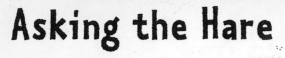

On midsummer night
when the grass is still
and the sea breathes out
and sleep-ghosts mutter

write your name
in cold washed sand
as a basking shark
sails past the Island,

then wait by the wall
silent, barefoot
in shivering starlight
wait and listen

the grass will stir
the grass will flatten,
look in the dark
where the grass flattens,

this is the hour
for asking the hare
she'll tell your fortune
if you don't hurt her,

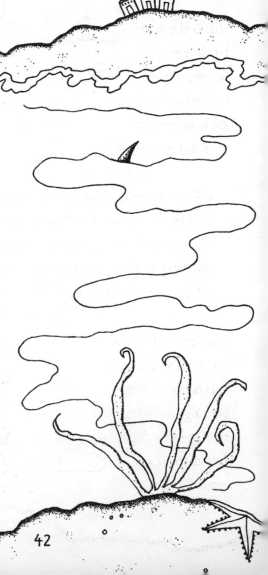

put out your hands
and she'll run into them
quivering, shivering,
big eyes burning,

this is the hour
to ask the hare,
for one minute
just around midnight
she'll answer any
question you ask her,

will my dad come home, will my mum let him in
will I like my school if we have to move
will my friends be my friends, will my life travel
will there still be forests and lakes and mountains
will the world be here in a hundred years,

just for one minute
just around midnight,
hold her shivering
burning, quivering
stretched for flight.
This is the hour
around midnight.

Helen Dunmore

His Dreams

The first night he dreamed his castle:
He dreamed the great, grey stones of it,
The moat of it, the towers of it,
The dank, dark dungeon hours of it.
The songs, the ancient wrongs of it,
The rats, the bats, the cats of it,
The dark of it, the doom of it,
The room on room on room of it,
And when he awoke, there was nothing.

The second night he dreamed his forest:
He dreamed the listening leaves of it,
The swings of it, the sways of it,
The rathless, pathless ways of it,
The old of it, the mould of it,
The owls, the prowls, the howls of it,
The dark of it, the dree of it,
The tree on tree on tree of it,
And when he awoke, there was nothing.

The third night he dreamed his ocean:
He dreamed the salty swell of it,
The sound, the taste and smell of it,
The oysters and the whales of it,
The serpents and the sea snails of it,
The reefs of it, the griefs of it,
The caverns and the graves of it,
The waves on waves on waves of it,
And when he awoke, there was nothing.

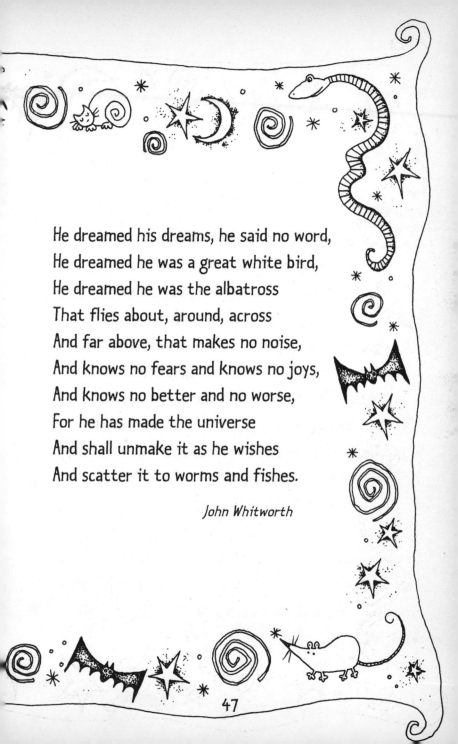

He dreamed his dreams, he said no word,
He dreamed he was a great white bird,
He dreamed he was the albatross
That flies about, around, across
And far above, that makes no noise,
And knows no fears and knows no joys,
And knows no better and no worse,
For he has made the universe
And shall unmake it as he wishes
And scatter it to worms and fishes.

John Whitworth

I am Taliesin.
I sing a perfect metre

I am Taliesin. I sing a perfect metre,
Which will last to the end of the world.
My patron is Elphin...

I know why there is an echo in a hollow;
Why silver gleams; why breath is black; why liver is bloody;
Why a cow has horns; why a woman is affectionate;
Why milk is white; why holly is green;
Why a kid is bearded; why the cow-parsnip is hollow;
Why brine is salt; why ale is bitter;
Why the linnet is green and berries red;
Why a cuckoo complains; why it sings;
I know where the cuckoos of summer are in winter.
I know what beasts there are at the bottom of the sea;
I know how many spears in battle; how many drops in a shower;
Why a river drowned Pharaoh's people;
Why fishes have scales,
Why a white swan has black feet...

I have been a blue salmon,
I have been a dog, a stag, a roebuck on the mountain,
A stock, a spade, an axe in the hand,
A stallion, a bull, a buck,
A grain which grew on a hill,
I was reaped, and placed in an oven,
I fell to the ground when I was being roasted
And a hen swallowed me.
For nine nights was I in her crop.
I have been dead, I have been alive,
I am Taliesin.

Taliesin

From
The Rubaiyat of
Omar Khayam

For in and out, above, below,
'Tis nothing but a magic shadow-show,
Played in a box whose candle is the sun
Round which we Phantom Figures come and go.

Edward Fitzgerald

From The Tempest

(From Act III, Scene II)

CALIBAN:
  Be not afeard; the isle is full of noises,
  Sounds and sweet airs, that give delight, and hurt not.
  Sometimes a thousand twangling instruments
  Will hum about mine ears; and sometime voices,
  That, if I then had wak'd after long sleep,
  Will make me sleep again: and then, in dreaming,
  The clouds methought would open, and show riches
  Ready to drop upon me; that, when I wak'd,
  I cried to dream again.

William Shakespeare

3
GHOSTS,
GHOULS and
MAGICAL
CREATURES

Hob-goblin

I am nothing-man
Dwelling in dark
Gobbling blackness into my guts
I choke in smoke
chewing up sooty bits
grinding up coals

I am hot-foot, coal-hopper, nip,
I stir the night's ashes with my heels

I am red-eyes, brittle-blaze
Cracking sparks at my finger-ends

All life long I listen to the purr of flames
And I spit my crackle back to their leaping hearts.

Berlie Doherty

From Goblin Market

Laughed every goblin
When they spied her peeping:
Came towards her hobbling,
Flying, running, leaping,
Puffing and blowing,
Chuckling, clapping, crowing,
Clucking and gobbling,
Mopping and mowing,
Full of airs and graces,
Pulling wry faces,
Demure grimaces,
Cat-like and rat-like,
Ratel- and wombat-like,
Snail-paced in a hurry,
Parrot-voiced and whistler,
Helter-skelter, hurry skurry,
Chattering like magpies,
Fluttering like pigeons,
Gliding like fishes.

Christina Rossetti

My Dad

My Dad's a werewolf.
No sweet little dear wolf,
All cuddly and snuffly
And perfectly luffly,
No. My Dad's a werewolf.
Your Dad can be near wolf,
All lumpy and stumpy,
All humpy and grumpy
All yell-and-you-jump-y,
All football-and-beer wolf,
But my Dad's a werewolf,
And, when the moon's full, he
Gets toothy and woolly,
Gets prowly and scowly,
Gets growly and howly,
Much more than a mere wolf,
A fill-you-with-fear wolf,
More ear-ful, more hair-ful.
You'd better be careful,
My Dad's a real werewolf.

John Whitworth

R. I. P.

Here resteth
Werewolf
Walter Witz
who chewed relations
into bits.
Aunties, uncles, nephews,
nieces,
all ended up

Ripped In Pieces.

Wes Magee

The Mermaids in the Sea

The mermaids in the sea are
Far hardier than we are;
And in the summer wear
Only the gilded air;
The blue translucencies
And foam-lace of the seas.
But when the seas are rough
They put on sailors' stuff:
Garments that seamen wore
Who never reached a shore.
They sit on rocks and crunch
An oceanic lunch.
They suck on bones and ribs,
They smack their salty lips
Above their sailor-bibs.

Gerda Mayer

The Ice Man

He slid into our classroom –
a six-foot man in a block of ice.
Cool, or what?
We stood him near the radiator –
a pool of water spread across the floor.

The tip of his nose,
the back of his hands,
then his shoulders began to show.
The water lapped around our feet.

Mark went home to get his swimming gear,
Sureya made a fleet of boats,
Esther floated up to the window.
Our teacher gave up on the Egyptians
and blew up a lilo.

Just before the water reached the top of the door
the Ice Man began to drink.
He slurped and gulped and swallowed and gurgled
until the room was dry.
Then he left as silently as he'd arrived.

There is a damp patch where he stood
which never goes away.

Chrissie Gittins

Scaly Skin

I have a toothsome evil grin
and blood around my lips and chin
that is of human origin.
It trickles down my scaly skin.

I've eyes as sharp as any pin.
They're hard and red and dark as sin.
I'm as roguish as Rasputin:
A devil in a scaly skin.

My roar's a deep explosive din
that mixes nitroglycerin
with flaming tongues of paraffin
so hot they scorch my scaly skin.

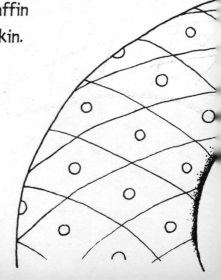

My cries that rise so high and thin
– like madness on a violin
or bagpipes with no discipline –
send shivers down my scaly skin.

But I've a toothsome evil grin
and blood around my lips and chin
that is of human origin.
It trickles down my scaly skin.

Nick Toczek

Dragon

Furnace fire
blow-torch
flame-thrower
fierce to scorch.
Spear-tail
terrible-claw
spiky-spine
dinosaur.
Flying fortress
comet-tail
starlight bright
on every scale.

Cave-dweller
cold as stone,
treasure-hoarder
all alone.
Centuries old,
short of breath,
eyes dimming,
close to death.
Lolling head,
faint groan,
soon to be
whitened bone

Penny Kent

Mr Alucard

Down our street there's someone new
Living next to the churchyard:
He is a man of mystery
Called Mr Alucard.
That's a strange name for starters,
But there's more that mystifies:
His wolfish grin, his sharp white teeth,
His very piercing eyes.
Wrapped in a big, black, batlike cloak
He goes out late at night
And I swear he casts no shadow
As he passes the street light.
Yesterday he said to me,
'What a lovely throat you've got',
And he stared and smiled a secret smile;
It worries me a lot.

There's something odd about his name...
I can't think what it is,
And I'd like to make some sense
Of those weird ways of his.
I definitely need some help,
So please try very hard
To help me solve the mystery
Of Mr Alucard.

Eric Finney

At Sunset

Men leave
The empty sepulchre,
Bewildered.

An owl hoots

As crosses,
Stakes
And mallets
Are gladly
Packed away.

Laughter.

Relief

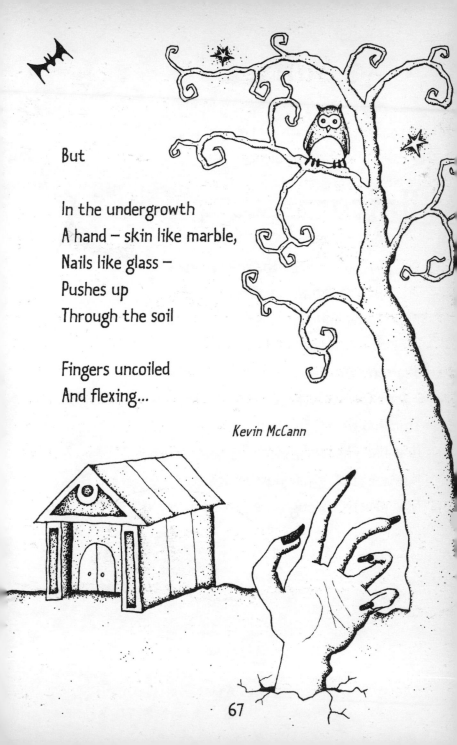

But

In the undergrowth
A hand – skin like marble,
Nails like glass –
Pushes up
Through the soil

Fingers uncoiled
And flexing...

Kevin McCann

Unicorn

My horn once drilled the inky night
My skin a Milky Way of white
None could hunt me, fast and wild...
Till I met a maiden undefiled
She rocked me in her snowdrop arms,
I slept too soon through all the charms
That hid her knife. Oh Unicorn!
Now like the lamb, you have been shorn:
Hunted; shot; this ghost so white
Now gallops through the groves of night.

Andrew Fusek Peters

Do Not Feed

Ogres are generally
ugly, unfriendly
and huge; especially
fond of the flesh
of a human or two
or three for tea.

Should not be annoyed.
Best to avoid.

Jill Townsend

On the Hallowe'en special

The ghosts pull hideous faces
That would make a mortal freeze
When the phantom bus conductor
Tolls the bell and wails 'Fears please!'

The ghosts would never dare try cheat
The phantom fear collector,
They're terrified of suffering
The wrath of the inspectre!

Philip Waddell

Green Man

I rise before you, man and tree
With rooted feet and eyes that see
Such leaves can harvest light from sun
Releasing water, oxygen:
Green is the balance, it helps us live
In a give and take land that's lost the give.
Trees in leaf are the lungs of the earth,
They give us air, the right of birth:
Voice in bark that's not yet gone,
Joined at the roots, you and I, we are one.

Polly Peters

Queen Nefertiti

Spin a coin, spin a coin,
    All fall down;
Queen Nefertiti
    Stalks through the town.

Over the pavements
    Her feet go clack
Her legs are as tall
    As a chimney stack;

Her fingers flicker
    Like snakes in the air,
The walls split open
    At her green-eyed stare;

Her voice is thin
    As the ghosts of bees;
She will crumble your bones,
    She will make your blood freeze.

Spin a coin, spin a coin,
    All fall down;
Queen Nefertiti
    Stalks through the town.

Anonymous

La belle Dame sans Merci

O, what can ail thee, knights at arms,
  Alone and palely loitering;
The sedge has withered from the lake,
  And no birds sing.

O, what can ail thee, knight at arms,
  So haggard and so woe-begone?
The squirrel's granary is full,
  And the harvest's done.

I see a lily on thy brow
  With anguish moist and fever-dew,
And on thy cheeks a fading rose
  Fast withereth too.

I met a lady in the meads,
    Full beautiful – a faery's child,
Here hair was long, her foot was light,
    And her eyes were wild.

I made a garland for her head,
    And bracelets too, and fragrant zone,
She looked at me as she did love,
    And made sweet moan.

I set her on my pacing steed
    And nothing else saw all day long;
For sideways would she lean, and sing
    A faery's song.

She found me roots of relish sweet,
    And honey wild and manna dew;
And sure in language strange she said –
    I love thee true.

She took me to her elfin grot,
    And there she gazed and sighed full sore:
And there I shut her wild wild eyes
    With kisses four.

And there she lullèd me asleep,
    And there I dreamed, ah woe betide,
The latest dream I ever dreamed
    On the cold hill side.

I saw pale kings and princes too,
  Pale warriors, death-pale were they all:
They cry'd – 'La belle Dame sans Merci
  Hath thee in thrall!'

I saw their starved lips in the gloam
  With horrid warning gapèd wide,
And I awoke, and found me here
  On the cold hill side.

And this is why I sojourn here
  Alone and palely loitering,
Though the sedge is withered from the lake,
  And no birds sing.

John Keats

From
A Midsummer Night's Dream

(From Act V, Scene I)

PUCK:
Now the hungry lion roars,
  And the wolf behowls the moon:
Whilst the heavy ploughman snores,
  All with weary task fordone.
Now the wasted brands do glow,
  Whilst the screech-owl, screeching loud,
Puts the wretch that lies in woe
  In remembrance of a shroud.
Now it is the time of night,
  That the graves all gaping wide,
Every one lets forth his sprite,
  In the church-way paths to glide.

And we fairies, that do run
  By the triple Hecate's team,
From the presence of the sun,
  Following darkness like a dream,
Now are frolic: not a mouse
Shall disturb this hallowed house.
I am sent with broom before,
To sweep the dust behind the door.

William Shakespeare

Here's to the Bean!

There's a baked bean imp
on the supermarket shelf,
a cheerful little fellow,
very happy with himself.

He zips along the aisles
in a whirl of orange spins,
he sings tomato pop songs
and tap dances on the tins.

He tightropes on the trolleys,
he tinkles on the tills
and croons Oh, how I love you!
to a pack of burger grills.

He's wicked, cool and up-to-date
as any bean can be;
low in salt, of course,
and absolutely
                sugar-free.

Patricia Leighton

The Fingal Dance

When they held a rave in Fingal's Cave
The Elfins danced with Joy
And Fred and Sal and Sid, their pal
And all that hoi-polloy.
They danced in line and they danced in pairs
And a ring-o'-roses that led to tears
When Morgan and the Organ and Hip the Harp
Played a hop and a jig in A Major sharp,
While the Leprachauns and Will-o'-the-wisps
Drank foxglove juice and crunched their crisps
'Til the early dawn, when they saw the light.
And a Faerie Sprite kissed a Troll 'Good Night'
And Rumpelstiltskin and Dwarfs galore –
(I am bad at maths, well, there might be more...
It's very difficult to keep score
While they dance about on the Fingal floor.)

Until ev'ryone fell asleep where they stood.
                        Well, they would...
And the Troll-catcher came with his horse and cart
And all the wee ravers would thus depart...

Robert D Hallmann

4
MYTHS and
LEGENDS

The Giant

Top-of-Beanstalk Dweller
Golden-Egg Collector
Coin Counter
Music Lover
Heavy Sleeper
Fe-Fi-Fo-Fum Shouter
Bone Grinder
Bread Baker
Jack Chaser
Poor Climber
Heavy Faller
Crater Maker

Damian Harvey

Fat is Not A Fairy Tale

I am thinking of a fairy tale,
Cinder Elephant,
Sleeping Tubby,
Snow Weight,
where the princess is not
anorexic, wasp-waisted,
flinging herself down the stairs.

I am thinking of a fary tale,
Hansel and Great
Repoundsel,
Bounty and the Beast,
where the beauty
has a pillowed breast,
and fingers plump as sausage.

I am thinking of a fairy tale
that is not yet written,
for a teller not yet born,
for a listener not yet conceived,
for a world not yet won,
where everything round is good:
the sun, wheels, cookies, and the princess.

Jane Yolen

Vishnu's Eagle

A sharp-beaked hunter of the chase,
Nemesis of the serpent race,
He scours the Earth, he straddles Space,

Spans the heavens with sturdy wings;
From worlds unseen, in glory brings
On his broad back the King of kings.

Debjani Chatterjee

White Horse

Horse on hill
Horse so still
Horse can't walk
Horse all chalk

Starry night
Moon so bright
Horse in sky
Horse can fly

No one know
No one see
Horse can roam
Horse so free

Fly by night
Stand by day
Horse half wish
Her life away

James Carter

Grimm Rules

There has to be a journey
past wolves and through thorny thickets.
Something must be endured.

The bad girl croaks out ravens,
Her loaves are stones. The good sister's
bread rises; words of peace turn into doves.

It's always the third son, the stupid one,
who pities the sour old woman.
The fool knows the answer to the riddle.

The right prince always gets the girl,
learns to play the system, finds out
just what it was she really wanted.

The evil witch knows her own oven
but cannot see what's under her nose.
She loses her three powers easily.

Justice must be done but not before
the glass mountain is scaled, the impossible
accomplished, the bloody shirt washed clean.

Angela Topping

Selchie

I

On a sand bank
Left high and drying
By the ebb tide
A woman sleeps

And a man's shadow
Brushes
The tongued-out halves
Of shellfish.

Strands of nibbled kelp.

He's reaching out

Slowly

Carefully

To snatch
A folded
Soft grey skin.

His to keep.

II

A hasty wedding.

Two sets of vows.

'I do...'

And

'After seven years
I'll set you free...'

And every day
While he takes
The boat out

She's searching
Frantically.

III
A woman running

And children look
For their mother

A woman running

And her husband
Stares down
At his sea-chest
Clawed open
And a soft skin,
Its colour drifting
With the tides,
Missing.

Gulls circle

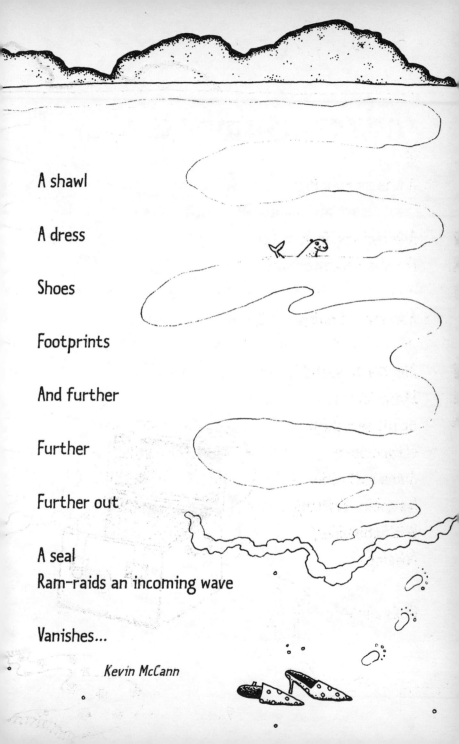

A shawl

A dress

Shoes

Footprints

And further

Further

Further out

A seal
Ram-raids an incoming wave

Vanishes...

Kevin McCann

Advertisement

Are your children peaky and thin?
Too many late nights? Too much telly?
Forest air and a fattening diet
   Will very soon put things right!

A week or two at Sweetmeat Cottage
Is bound to make them scrumptiously chubby.
Children just love my gingerbread house,
   My liquorice doors and chimneys.

There's everything here to delight a child,
And one kind lady to see to their needs –
For I love children, tasty little darlings!
   Apply without delay.

Gerard Benson

Cautionary rhymes for young dragons

Little Miss Dragon sat on her wagon
Painting her claws bright red.
A helmeted rider
Sat down beside her,
Took his sword out and chopped off her head.

John Foster

Limerick

A dark-haired young princess was fond
Of kissing a frog in the pond.
But it made the frog wince
'Cos he wasn't a prince,
And besides, he wanted a blonde.

Mike Jubb

Flesh Creeper

When the moon is the merest sliver,
And thousands of stars stab the sky,
When Grandfather Toad comes crawling,
So do I.

When there's hardly a sound from the river,
And bats begin to fly,
When the Willow Wolf comes prowling,
So do I.

When even the shadows shiver,
And statues start to cry,
When the Old Owl of Merda comes hunting,
So do I.

So do I.

Mike Jubb

A Potholer tells his Story

The summer was bone dry. We knew a cave
Where water nearly touched the roof;
Only the stupid or the very brave
Would try their luck. But we had certain proof
That dry caves lay beyond and with the drought
It might be possible to scramble through.
We swam at first, but when we were about
Half a mile in the ceiling dropped. We knew
The danger, but on we went. Luckily
We soon found air. That's where we found them, stark
And cold. Our light went out. We couldn't see
Them, but we heard them moving in the dark,
Clanking their swords. We shivered, dripping wet,
And then an echo shook the cave: 'Not yet!'

David Orme

Merlin

He's the green of the woods
The voice in your head
The sound of your words
  As yet unsaid
The bird on the wing
The fish in the stream
The demon that stalks
  Your deepest dream
The gossamer web
The rain on the leaf

The vixen at birth
  The Raynard thief
The stone in the circle
The snake in the grass
The Solstice the Equinox
  Seasons that pass
Your dearest desire
Your hunger your thirst
He's all. He is nothing
  The last and the first...

Karen Bowman

A Close Shave

Hubble
bubble
toil
and
trouble
Merlin
shaved
his
beard
off
now
he's
got
designer
stubble!

Steve Fisher

The Cyclops' Revenge

Hear me, Poseidon,
hail-thrower, wave-maker,
brewer of foam and flood,
great god of the sea!
Send me winds, send me rain,
send me hurricane, storm;
send me tempests too black
for the skies to contain!
May Charybdis' wild waters
hiss with your fury,
close round Odysseus
and his fine men;
may they lurch from their ships
may they sink to your sands;
may they never set foot
on their own lands
again!

Judith Nicholls

Excalibur

I am carrying his sword,
arm's-length through the dark wood.
In the rear, two armies dead,
Arthur dying.

Glittering, finest in the world,
on its hilt two serpents coiled,
precious stones in beaten gold.
Throw away the sword.

At half-light, reach the lake,
hear the small waves break
and the wind in the reeds.
No, I saw nothing.

Get back, to find him coughing blood
(not one dram of what was spilled),
knights gone to the sandy ground,
women to convents.

He will find out, and rage.
Do what the rule-book says,
look towards a later age.
They will glorify him.

Keep before their eyes the gold,
the song, the glamour of the blade,
and dry bones stick through Arthur's shroud.
Throw away the sword.

All dead, I alone
to keep the legend riding on.
And the sword winks in the white sun.
Throw it.

Merryn Williams

5
TWILIGHT

Magic Everywhere

Magic in an
ice cream
moonbeam
sweet dream
Magic in a
mountain stream
Magic everywhere

Magic in a
birthday
school day
sun ray
magic in a
bob sleigh
Magic at the fair

Magic in a
disco light
midnight
pillow fight
Magic in a
flying kite
Magic in the air

Magic in a
bus trip
hot chip
pool dip
Magic in a
friendship
Magic is to share

Jim Hatfield

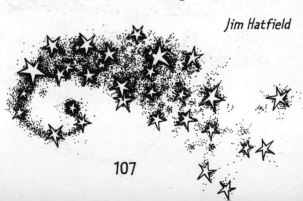

Crow's Nest

Lights out across the bedroom,
shadows on the wall,
lights out across the garden,
darkness on the lawn.
Lights out across the common
and the stream and the track,
lights out across the bay,
and the sea turns to black.
And the moon rises slowly
in a purple night sky,
and the waves whisper softly
as a shadow shivers by.

Lights out across the bedroom,
and the shadows gathering
are from a keel upon the black sea
and sails that spread like wings,
with moonlight in the rigging
and elf-light on the deck,

and drunken sailors dancing
to a tune in the crow's nest.
Played by a ship's lad,
who spins magic in his mind,
the walls around his bed
are the shore he left behind.

The sun comes up for morning
on the walls and in the bay,
and the black sea turns to ash
and the sail boat fades away.
And the sleeper wakes from dreaming
of a life adventuring,
and the tune he played has gone
just like a gift of conjuring.
And the lad who sits at breakfast
with his school bag by his side,
has come freshly from a crow's nest,
blinking magic from his eyes.

Pauline Fisk

Change

Who cast a spell on my grandad
To make him lose his mind;
To make him rude and nasty
When he used to be so kind?

Which wizard stole my grandad's brain,
And sailed it far away
Till he recalls long, long ago;
Forgets just yesterday?

Which witch robbed him of his legs
That used to walk him miles?
What spell-bound words reduce to tears
His face once flowered with smiles?

Is there a wizard or witch
To answer for this crime?
Or is the only culprit
The womb to tomb of time?

John Kitching

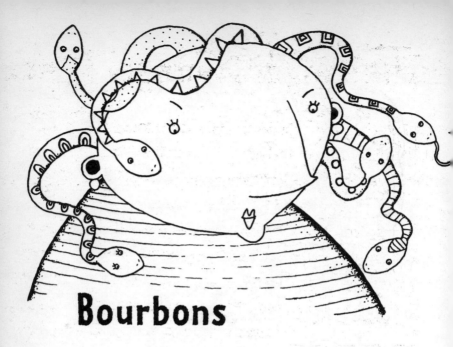

Bourbons

My little brother thought
That the scary ladies
With evil eyes
And snakes in their hair
Were called
Bourbons.

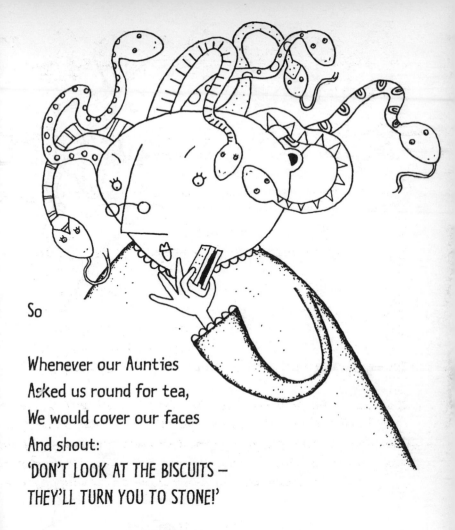

So

Whenever our Aunties
Asked us round for tea,
We would cover our faces
And shout:
'DON'T LOOK AT THE BISCUITS –
THEY'LL TURN YOU TO STONE!'

And our angry Aunties
Would glare at us
Like GORGONS.

Clare Bevan

The Song of Wandering Aengus

I went out to the hazel wood,
Because a fire was in my head,
And cut and peeled a hazel wand,
And hooked a berry to a thread;
And when white moths were on the wing,
And moth-like stars were flickering out,
I dropped the berry in a stream
And caught a little silver trout.

When I had laid it on the floor
I went to blow the fire aflame,
But something rustled on the floor,
And some one called me by my name;

It had become a glimmering girl
With apple blossom in her hair
Who called me by my name and ran
And faded through the brightening air.

Though I am old with wandering
Through hollow lands and hilly lands,
I will find out where she has gone,
And kiss her lips and take her hands;
And walk among long dappled grass,
And pluck till time and times are done
The silver apples of the moon,
The golden apples of the sun.

W B Yeats

Hazel

Sing magic of the hazel,
its bark of reddish-brown,
its yellow lambs'-tail catkins
where the pollen seeds float down.

Sing magic of the hazel
whose bending form allows
a witch, for an enchanted wand,
to cut and peel its boughs.

Sing magic of the hazel
whose forked twigs, wavering,
detect rich metals underground,
divine a water spring.

Sing magic of the hazel.
Its nuts, dropped down a well,
made dappled spots on salmon
who were feeding where they fell.

Sing magic of the hazel,
its filberts sweet and good,
its concentrated energy
the wisdom of the wood.

Alison Chisholm

Amazing Grace

My mate Grace is totally magic,
She swallows secrets without a blink.
And when she utters dead rude spells,
She can make a bully shrink!
She's a witch of words! In a flurry of tears,
With a huff and a puff, he disappears!

My mate Grace is totally magic,
I bet she's psychic! Don't you knock it!
From over a hundred metres away,
She senses chocolate in my pocket
Even though I might be famished,
With a flash of her teeth, Kaboom! It's vanished!

My mate Grace is totally magic,
Doubt disappears in the world she inhabits;
In lessons, her brain is a huge top hat,
Answers hop from her head like rabbits!
Her pen is the wand of the spelling test,
With a flourish, she conjures and comes out best.

My mate Grace is totally magic,
A witch on the pitch, she likes to tell us
She even beats me, it's utterly tragic!
But she is a girl, so I can't be jealous...
And I'd better watch out I don't turn into a frog,
'Cos she might trick me into giving her a snog!!!

Andrew Fusek Peters

A Girl's Head

In it there is a dream
that was started
before she was born,

and there is a globe
with hemispheres
which shall be happy.

There is her own spacecraft,
a chosen dress
and pictures of her friends.

There are shining rings
and a maze of mirrors.

There is a diary
for surprise occasions.

There is a horse springing hooves
across the sky.

There is a sea that
tides and swells
and cannot be mapped.

There is untold hope
in that no equation exactly
fits a head.

> Katherine Gallagher
> (After the poem, 'A Boy's Head'
> by Miroslav Holub)

Night-Spell

Close your eyes
    and wish for light
to chase away
    the net of night.

The stars are only
    down the street,
and deep in sleep
    it's there we'll meet.

Rest your head
    and dream till dawn,
in sleep be free
    as a fleet-foot fawn.

The stars are only
  down the street,
and deep in sleep
  it's there we'll meet.

Take into sleep
  this night-spell charm
to set you safe
  against all harm.

The stars are only
  down the street,
and deep in sleep
  it's there we'll meet.

John Rice

The Song of Enchantment

A Song of Enchantment I sang me there,
In a green-green wood, by waters fair,
Just as the words came up to me
I sang it under the wild wood tree.

Widdershins turned I, singing it low,
Watching the wild birds come and go;
No cloud in the deep dark blue to be seen
Under the thick-thatched branches green.

Twilight came; silence came;
The planet of evening's silver flame;
By darkening paths I wandered through
Thickets trembling with drops of dew.

But the music is lost and the words are gone
Of the song I sang as I sat alone,
Ages and ages have fallen on me –
On the wood and the pool and the elder tree.

Walter de la Mare

Kubla Khan

In Xanadu did Kubla Khan
A stately pleasure-dome decree:
Where Alph, the sacred river, ran
Through caverns measureless to man
   Down to a sunless sea.
So twice five miles of fertile ground
With walls and towers were girdled round:
And here were gardens bright with sinuous rills,
Where blossomed many an incense-bearing tree;
And here were forests ancient as the hills,
Enfolding sunny spots of greenery.

But oh! that deep romantic chasm which slanted
Down the green hill athwart a cedarn cover!
A savage place! as holy and enchanted
As e'er beneath a waning moon was haunted
By woman wailing for her demon-lover!

And from this chasm, with ceaseless turmoil seething,
As if this earth in fast thick pants were breathing,
A mighty fountain momently was forced:
Amid whose swift half-intermitted burst
Huge fragments vaulted like rebounding hail,
Or chaffy grain beneath the thresher's flail:
And 'mid these dancing rocks at once and ever
It flung up momently the sacred river.
Five miles meandering with a mazy motion
Through wood and dale the sacred river ran,
Then reached the caverns measureless to man,
And sank in tumult to a lifeless ocean:
And 'mid this tumult Kubla heard from far
Ancestral voices prophesying war!

   The shadow of the dome of pleasure
   Floated midway on the waves;
   Where was heard the mingled measure
   From the fountain and the caves.
It was a miracle of rare device,
A sunny pleasure-dome with caves of ice!

A damsel with a dulcimer
In a vision once I saw:
It was an Abyssinian maid,
And on her dulcimer she played,
Singing of Mount Abora.
Could I revive within me
Her symphony and song,
To such a deep delight 'twould win me,
That with music loud and long,
I would build that dome in air,
That sunny dome! those caves of ice!
And all who heard should see them there,
And all should cry, Beware! Beware!
His flashing eyes, his floating hair!
Weave a circle round him thrice,
And close your eyes with holy dread,
For he on honey-dew hath fed,
And drunk the milk of Paradise.

Samuel Taylor Coleridge

A Feather from an Angel

Anton's box of treasures held
a silver key and a glassy stone,
a figurine made of polished bone
and a feather from an angel.

The figurine was from Borneo,
the stone from France or Italy,
the silver key was a mystery
but the feather came from an angel.

We might have believed him if he'd said
the feather fell from a bleached white crow
but he always replied, 'It's an angel's, I know,
a feather from an angel.'

We might have believed him if he'd said,
'An albatross let the feather fall,'
But he had no doubt, no doubt at all,
his feather came from an angel.

'I thought I'd dreamt him one night,' he'd say,
'But in the morning I knew he'd been there;
he left a feather on my bedside chair,
a feather from an angel.'

And it seems that all my life I've looked
for the sort of belief that nothing could shift,
something simple and precious as Anton's gift,
a feather from an angel.

Brian Moses

The Curtain

When the curtain goes down at the end of the play,
The actors and actresses hurry away.

Titania, Bottom, and Quince, being stars,
Can afford to drive home in their own private cars.

Hippolyta, Starveling, and Flute are in luck,
They've been offered a lift in a taxi by Puck;

And Snug and Lysander and Oberon pop
In a bus, and Demetrius clambers on top.

With the chorus of fairies no bus can compete,
So they are obliged to trudge home on their feet:

It seems rather hard on the poor little things,
After flying about all the evening with wings.

Guy Boas

From The Tempest

(From Act IV, Scene I)

PROSPERO:

  As if you were dismay'd: be cheerful, sir:
  Our revels now are ended: these our actors,
  As I fortold you, were all spirits, and
  Are melted into air, into thin air:
  And, like the baseless fabric of this vision
  The cloud-capp'd towers, the gorgeous palaces,
  The solemn temples, the great globe itself,
  Yea, all which it inherit, shall dissolve,
  And like this insubstantial pageant faded,
  Leave not a rack behind: We are such stuff
  As dreams are made of, and our little life
  Is rounded with a sleep. – Sir, I am vex'd;
  Bear with my weakness; my old brain is troubled,
  Be not disturb'd with my infirmity;
  If you be pleased, retire into my cell,
  And there repose; a turn or two I'll walk,
  To still my beating mind.

William Shakespeare

6
CURSES,
CHARMS
and SPELLS

A Magic Spell

Someone ☆ade some of the lett☆rs

Disappear f☆om the ☆ines of th☆s poem,

Ca☆ you guess who?

Steve Fisher

133

Have you heard...?

'There'll be rane and sno
And sleat for ever.'
(Oh no – not MORE
Bad spells of weather...!)

Trevor Harvey

Spelling Test

A spell to turn someone into a striped
   horse-like creature... **Zebra**cadabara
Spell to change someone into a clawed sideways-
   walking crustacean... **Crab**racadabra
Spell to do your shopping for you... **Asda**cadabra
Spell that takes pictures... Abrada**camera**
Spell that makes you hiss and writhe on your belly...
   Abrada**cobra**
Spell that lights up a very old-fashioned and
   well-to-do ballroom... Abra**candelabra**
Spell that bashes your sister... Abrada**clobberer**
Spell that bashes your brother... Abrada**clobberim**
Spell that makes your teacher cross... Abra**mad**abra
Spell to make you cheerful... Abra**glad**abra
Really rude underwear spell... **Abra**cada**bra**
Spell to make you fall over... *Izzy whizzy let's get dizzy*
Bubbling frothing spell... *Izzy whizzy let's get fizzy*
Spell that interrupts the poet halfway through
   a wo**SHAZAM**rd.

Paul Cookson

A spell to take you to the top of the class

Minor to major,
Little to lot,
Simple to sager,
Lukewarm to hot.

Crypt up to spire,
Heel up to head,
Dazzler from dire,
Gold out of lead.

Bridge up from galley,
Topper from tail,
High Street from alley,
Hammer from nail.

Plodder to athlete,
Fizzle to POP,
Turn the result sheet
So bottom comes top.

Philip Waddell

A spell for enchanting feet

(This powerful spell really works!)

If your feet smell like Camemberts
Take your boots (the smelly pairs
Complete with tongues and eyes for laces)
And bear them off a thousand paces.
Now stuffed well with your smelly socks
Inter them – deep – in a lead-lined box.
Retrace your steps and wash your feet
Now have a sniff – don't they smell sweet!

Philip Waddell

From
A Midsummer Night's Dream

(From Act III, Scene II)

OBERON:
Flower of this purple dye,
Hit with Cupid's archery,
Sink in apple of his eye.
When his love he doth espy,
Let her shine as gloriously
As the Venus of the sky.
When thou wakest, if she be by,
Beg of her for remedy.

William Shakespeare

Charming

The well-groomed woman
held my hand
Rubbed warm fingers
Over the wart
And whispered,
There we are.

There we are?
Is that it? I thought,
Disappointed that no
Black-robed crone
Had dragged me to
Her bubbling cauldron
And held me under
Prattling arcane spells
As claps of thunder
Rattled round the room.

I felt no different
As we walked down the hill
To the car park.
But I glanced at my hand
A week later
And the wart
Had vanished.

Roger Stevens

Pimple Potion Number Nine

Do you seek a simple pimple
or a double-dimpled wart,
with one long hair, in the middle,
maybe several – black and short?
I've a notion that this potion
can bring spots or zits in zillions
plus battalions of verrucas
(snooker-ball-sized, bright vermilion).

Blackheads, bunions, boils, big freckles,
choice carbuncles, crusty corns...
Shake the bottle: check the dosage;
give to victims, night and morn.
Guaranteed to be effective,
yes, I can safely say,
not an ocean of blotch lotion
could wash the splotch away.
Try some! Buy some! You'll be fine –
Pimple Potion Number Nine.

Mike Johnson

143

A Spell for Love

I wove this simple spell to see
If our love could ever be.
I spoke her name, Samantha Grimes,
Exactly seventy-seven times;
Her picture that adorns my wall
(On the class photo, rather small):
I kissed it seventeen times an hour;
I felt my love spell gather power.
And now my charm's essentials were
Three objects that belonged to her.
Difficult this, but first I'd found
A hairclip she'd dropped on the ground
And then I managed to include
A pencil that she'd partly chewed
And a yoghurt pot she'd thrown away
After school dinner yesterday.
Lastly her writing... I had it, yes!
A note to me saying Get lost. S.

Over these items, seven times
I chanted, 'Love me do, Sam Grimes.'
With these ingredients for my spell
Beneath my pillow, I slept well,
Confident that this charm's strong power
Would cause a lasting love to flower.

Morning – the vital assignation
And at it this brief conversation:
'Samantha, could you love me?
And please – no ifs or buts.'
'My pencil and hairclip, please.
You pinch my things. You're nuts.'

Eric Finney

From King Lear

(Act III, Scene II)

LEAR:
  Blow winds and crack your cheeks! Rage, Blow!
  You cataracts and hurricanes, spout
  Till you have drenched our steeples, drown'd the cocks!
  You sulph'rous and thought-executing fires,
  Vaunt-couriers of oak-cleaving thunderbolts,
  Singe my white head! And thou, all shaking thunder,
  Strike flat the thick rotundity o' th' world!
  Crack nature's moulds, all germens spill at once
  That makes ingrateful man!

William Shakespeare

A Charm

O wen, wen, O little wennikins,
Here shall you build not, here have no abode,
But you must northwards to the nearby hill,
For there, O wretched one, you have a brother,
And he shall lay a leaf upon your head.
Under wolf's foot and under eagle's wing,
'Neath claw of eagle ever may you fade.
May you decrease like coal upon the hearth,
Shrivel away like dirt upon the wall,
Evaporate like water in a pail,
Become as little as a linseed-grain,
Much smaller than a hand-worm's hip-bone is,
And so diminish that you come to nothing.

Anonymous
From the Anglo-Saxon
(translated by Richard Hamer)

Kylie's Curse on Kevin Spritely

May your brain become a sponge
And your nostrils flow with gunge
Swap some baked beans for those eyes
That flattered me with cunning lies.
If this spell now serves me well,
May your feet begin to smell
So bad the school evacuates,
And the stench kills off your mates.
Hear my curse, now do I pray
That Mr Bad Breath comes to stay
And girls run off eternally
To pay you back for ditching me.

Andrew Fusek Peters

From
The Tempest

(From Act I, Scene II)

CALIBAN:

> As wicked dew as e'r my mother brush'd
> With raven's feather from unwholesome fen
> Drop on you both! A south-west blow on ye
> And blister you all o'er!

William Shakespeare

Spell

By cone and resin of the tree
By the snail's house and the shining way,
By mouth of bird and hollow bone,
White, secret root and mossy stone,
Cold eye of snake and cat's rough tongue,
Drunkard's whisper, idiot's song;
By the red hearth and milky frost,
Sticky bud, leaf tempest-tossed,
By my quaking flesh and cold
Cruel purpose, by the old
Intolerance of tired eyes
And insolence of curious boys;
By this bitter of the rind,
Love's sweet centre I can bind.

Bruce Barr

THE
END

Index by title

Index by author

Acknowledgements

The editor and publishers gratefully acknowledge permission to reproduce the following copyright material:

Bruce Barr for 'Spell';

David Bateman for 'Matchbox';

Catherine Benson for 'Witch Villanelle';

Gerard Benson (under the pseudonym C J D Doyle) for 'Advertisement', from **This Poem Doesn't Rhyme** (Puffin), 1991;

Clare Bevan for 'Abrabadabra Alphabet' and 'Bourbons';

Karen Bowman for 'Merlin';

Curtis Brown, Ltd for 'Fat Is Not a Fairy Tale' by Jane Yolen from **Such a Pretty Face** (Meisha-Merlin Publishing Co), 1999;

James Carter for 'White Horse';

Debjani Chatterjee for 'Vishnu's Eagle' from **Albino Gecko** (University of Salzburg Press) 1998;

Alison Chisholm for 'Hazel';

Paul Cookson for 'Wizard with the Ball' and 'Spelling Test';

Jennifer Curry for 'A Country Spell Against Witches';

Berlie Doherty for 'Hob-Goblin' and 'Witch and Wizard';

David Duncombe and Berlie Doherty for 'Wizard and Witch';

Eric Finney for 'Mr Alucard' and 'A Spell for Love';

Steve Fisher for 'You'll like this, not a lot!', 'A Close Shave' and 'A Magic Spell';

Pauline Fisk for 'Crow's Nest';

John Foster for 'Cautionary Rhymes for Young Dragons', 2003;

Andrew Fusek Peters for 'Amazing Grace' from **My Gang, Poems about Friendship** (Macmillan), 'Kylie's Curse on Kevin Spritely' and 'Unicorn';

Katherine Gallagher for 'A Girl's Head (after the poem, 'A Boy's Head' by Miroslav Holub), from **Fish-Rings on Water** (Forest Books), 1989;

Chrissie Gittins for 'The Ice Man';

Robert D Hallmann for 'The Fingal Dance';

Damian Harvey for 'The Giant';

Trevor Harvey for 'Have you heard...?';

Jim Hatfield for 'Magic Everywhere';

Mike Johnson for 'Pimple Potion Number Nine';

Mike Jubb for 'The Sorceror's Dentist', 'Flesh Creeper' and 'Limerick';

Penny Kent for 'Dragon';

John Kitching for 'Change';

Patricia Leighton for 'Here's to the Bean!';

Patrick J Lewis for 'The Magician's Hands', from **Cricket Magazine** (November 1995 issue);

The Literary Trustees of Walter de la Mare and the Society of Authors as their representative for 'The Ride-By-Nights' and 'The Song of Enchantment';

Kevin McCann for 'At Sunset' and 'Selchie';

Wes Magee for 'R.I.P.';

Gerda Mayer for 'The Mermaids in the Sea', from **'The Poetry Review'** [comp. 'Not Just Kids' Stuff'], 1993;

Brian Moses for 'A Feather from an Angel';

Judith Nicholls for 'The Cyclops' Revenge' from **'Dragonsfire'** (Faber & Faber), 1990;

David Orme for 'A Potholer tells his Story' from **'A Magic Nation'**, 2002;

Gareth Owen for 'The Magician' from **'Collected Poems for Children'** (Macmillan);

Polly Peters for 'Green Man';

Punch, Ltd for 'The Curtain' by Guy Boas;

John Rice for 'Night-Spell';

Matt Simpson for 'An Autumn Ghost';

Roger Stevens for 'Magic Mat' and 'Charming';

Nick Toczek for 'Scaly Skin';

Shirley Tomlinson for 'Buckle Shoe Dance';

Angela Topping for 'The Fiddle' (Stride), 1999 and 'Grimm Rules';

Jill Townsend for 'Alchemy' and 'Do Not Feed';

Philip Waddell for 'Hell's Angel', 'On the Hallowe'en special', 'A spell to take you to the top of the class', 'A spell for enchanting feet' and 'Haiku';

A P Watt Ltd for 'The Song of Wondering Aengus' by Michael B Yeats;

A P Watt Ltd for 'Asking the Hare' by Helen Dunmore;

Colin West for 'The Wizard and the Lizard' from **'A Step in the Wrong Direction'** (Hutchinson), 1984;

John Whitworth for 'His Dreams' and 'My Dad';

Merryn Williams for 'Excalibur'.

While every effort has been made to obtain permission, there may still be cases in which we have failed to trace a copyright holder. The publisher will be happy to correct any omission in future reprintings.

Andrew Fusek Peters is 'an experienced and accomplished anthologist'.
Times Educational Supplement

'His anthologies are always surprising and interesting.'
Books for Keeps

The Unidentified Frying Omelette 'is an excellent anthology and glossary of verse forms, both useful and fun'.
Signal

'It is rare and welcome to find a collection (*Poems with Attitude*) that speaks so directly to teenagers.'
The Guardian

Together with Polly Peters, Andrew Fusek Peters has written and edited over thirty books for young people, many critically acclaimed. Their collection of teenage poetry – *Poems With Attitude* – has become a bestseller. Andrew also visits schools countrywide, performing his poems and stories and playing a mean didgeridoo. Find out more about his books and music on www.tallpoet.com